The BRAVE Life

Bold. Resilient. Authentic. Victorious. Empowered

What to Do When Life Scares the Faith Out of You

Takima Howze

First Printing, 2016
ISBN 0-9000000-0-0

Takima Howze
Bronx, NY 10460
www.TakimaHWrites.com

Printed in the United States of America

Dedications

My Abba:
You have done it again! You have poured into me so that I can pour into them—my dear readers. You have given to me so I can give to them. You have made me *Bold, Resilient, Authentic, Victorious*, and *Empowered* so I can show them how to be. I am FOREVER Yours, Abba!

My Baby girl, Victorya Joi:
This book is a testament of what you have taught me in your 5 years of being here with me. Each year with you has laid the foundation in me for my Boldness, Resiliency, Authenticity, Victory, and Empowerment. Without you, I could not be BRAVE. I Love You!

And to those who...
are struggling in life right NOW. I know what it feels like to be afraid and not know your own abilities to live the best life designed for you. I dedicate this book to you because the fact that you are reading it, proves that you are Already BRAVE!

Acknowledgments

To my Family:
My Mothers — Josephine Howze & Pearl Bowles. Thank You for having me, molding me and teaching me the importance of Love, Sacrifice, and Redemption.

My siblings — Wayne Scott, Mark Scott, Jodi Scott, Shaun Artis, Stephane Howze, Tyeese Howze, Tina Howze, Nakaiya Bowles, & my heart Jamel Bailey. Thank you all so much for supporting me, loving me and always cheering me on and my dreams! I love You ALL beyond the amount of words I can write!

My nieces and nephews — You all inspire me to be great and to strive to be an example that you will be honored to follow.

My cousins, aunts, uncles, grandparents, your love and support means everything to me.

To My Friends:
(You all know who you are)
Thank You for always supporting my dreams even when it didn't make sense and you thought I was CRAZY! :)

To My Mentors:
Kym Williams & Dajuan Williams — Thank you for always believing in me and my capabilities. For always instilling in me the importance of keeping God first and still helping me to make "grits", I appreciate you!

Tamika Sims — Thank you for being my midwife and pushing me to be everything that was already in me. Thank you for never giving up on me and challenging me to take myself and my writing and words to the next level!

Yvonne Baxter — Thank you for accepting me and for making me take a "job" when I didn't want it. It turned out to be what I NEEDED to get to where I am today. Your love for me is insurmountable!

Nicole Henningham — You will always be my Elijah! I love you!

Special Thanks To:
Allison Arnett — You are an angel and such a talented graphic artist! My book covers and flyers will ALWAYS be top notch because of you!

My Bethel Gospel Assembly Family, My Christian Cultural Center Family, My One Accord Dance Ministry Family. Thank You for your prayers and love!

Very Special Thank You to My Readers! My prayer is that you will ALWAYS be BRAVE at ALL TIMES!

I LOVE YOU ALL!

The B.R.A.V.E. Contents

BRAVE Letter to Reader

My Dear BRAVESoul,

I am so honored to be able to write this book! When God placed this on my heart to write, I was happy and truly excited at first. I flowed right through the first two chapters without hesitation. As I got to the third, there was a halt.

I did not understand why because I was so sure of what I was supposed to write, I knew God wanted me to write this book but I faced a serious case of Fear aka "writer's block". Now you may ask, "How can you be fearful and you are writing a book on being BRAVE"? Well, I am so glad you asked me! Being BRAVE doesn't always mean being willing, open and READY to do or accomplish every task you have been set out to do. You can be BRAVE and experience fear, hesitation, doubt but what makes you BRAVE is the willingness to recognize what you feel and do it ANYWAY!

I realized I was fearful because things in my personal life started to get really challenging and I did not know how to handle it. I often found myself questioning what I was called to do because things in my life weren't as perfect as I wanted them to be. I soon found out that, that is exactly what qualified me to write this book and that I needed to write it more than ever.

This book is less about me and more about you. Everything I experience and go through is purposed for me to write about so that I can help you to Be BRAVE and Live BRAVE!

What I pray that you will get out of this book is not only inspiration but that you will be able to put together a strategy that will help you to Be Bold, Resilient, Authentic, Victorious & Empowered in the midst of the trial, challenge, or struggle you are facing. There is a way out and there is no better way than The BRAVE Way!
See you on the BRAVE Side!

I Love you and always remember,
Be You, Stay True and Live BRAVE!

Takima Howze

1

BE Bold

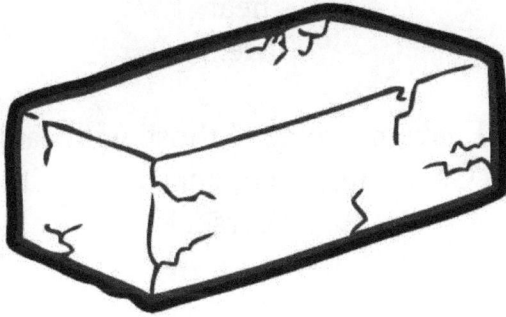

"Not Hesitating or fearful in the face of actual or possible danger or rebuff; courageous and daring."

Poem
Hiding...

Bottled up and hiding,
dark corners with no one to spy
Is it mouth closed, words ready, to
spill forth like a fountain…

No One
Wants
to
hear
Me…

I have no voice to those with ears.
Chattering teeth, consumed with
Fears...

Can
You
See
Me?

Bold Faith
"And the (Bold) shall walk by faith."

Being a Christian requires a lot of denouncing who you think you are. Don't believe me? Ask any Christian who came to Christ as timid, loud, submissive, or abrasive. They are now outspoken, quiet when necessary, open, and more humble. The flip side to this is telling people and sharing with them that you are a Christian.

In society today, when you tell someone you are a Christian, you are immediately slapped on a label that reads: "Jesus Freak" or "Beware, Judgment Ahead!" Not so much a positive poster sign of declaration, right? Like most who wear that sign and cover it up, what do you think God feels about us "shrinking back"?

"But we do not belong to those who shrink back and are destroyed, but to those who have faith and are saved." – Hebrews 10:29

The Bible is clear about us confessing our faith BOLDLY to others. Christ reminds us:

"But everyone who denies me here on earth, I will also deny before my Father in heaven" (Matthew 10:33).

I don't know about you, but I sure do not want to be denied by Christ when He returns. Let me tell you how I learned how to be Bold in my faith.

A scary new Christian experience...

When I first became saved, I was a member of a church that was very big on "sharing your faith." Now, with me being new to the faith, I did not understand this zeal of making sure to tell everyone about my newfound faith in Christ. I thought becoming a Christian was, you learned about Christ, you learned the "Do's and Don'ts" and you lived your life happily ever after, Amen. Am I alone in this? Well, very soon, I learned being a Christian was more than carrying the name, there was work to be done.

This church in particular made it a point that all the members "shared our faith" a certain amount of times every week. At first, I was like, "oh ya'll are crazy, I don't go up to strangers! Haven't you heard of Stranger Danger?!" I quickly learned and understood why I needed to do it but I did not necessarily agree with the method in which they taught us to do it.

To me, I always felt like if I did not go up to a stranger and talk to someone, God would be mad at me or something. I was honestly terrified of doing so, I wasn't trying to be a rebellious "babe in Christ" (not all the time anyway). Imagine you walking up to strangers every day and asking them, "Hey, do you know Jesus? Well, if you don't, You NEED Him! Can I invite you to my church?" I was a bonafide Weirdo! I will be honest, if someone approached me like that, I would engage them and keep it pushing with no follow-up, and we HAD to follow up.

This was to "prove" that we spoke to people and that we were bringing people to our church every Sunday.

That experience made me feel leery about talking to people about my faith, my association with the church or even my relationship with Christ. Later in life (when I left the church), I would not mention my Christianity unless someone made the statement first. I vowed to not be one of those "soapbox" preaching Christians on the train or on the sidewalks. You would not find me talking about "Jesus is coming, REPENT." Nope, not for me.

As I grew in my Christian walk and began to understand more about God and what it truly meant to 1. Have faith and 2. Share my faith, I understood it was less about just randomly going up to people and asking them, "Hey, do you know Jesus? Let me pray with your soul out of hell." Building relationships with people, engaging in conversation, letting them see my life, and sharing how I could be going through so much and still smile and have joy on the inside, that is how you really share your faith with people and with Boldness.

Having Bold Faith

Bold faith is the foundation of you being bold in every area of your entire life. It literally means, *"In the same way, let your light shine before others, that they may see your good deeds and glorify your Father in heaven"* (Matthew 5:16).

We should never be ashamed of the light within us, which is Christ Jesus. He created us with His light and He expects us to let it shine! (Don't make me break out in the song "This little light of mine"!) We were not meant to hide it, cover it up or even shut up about Him or the things that He has done for us. That is why telling our stories and testimonies are essential in being a Christian.

How Bold is your Faith?

Answer this...

When people ask if you are a Christian especially in present day society, do you do any of the following?

1. You Boldly and Proudly say "YES"!
2. You say "Yes" reluctantly like "Yeah, but I am not one of those Jesus Freaks"
3. You simply and tactically avoid the question.
4. You're like Peter and deny your connection with Christ (It's okay if you do, no judgment! That's why you are reading this book! You are gonna be BOLD in Your Faith).

If your answer was:

1.   You are BOLD, Loud and Proud!
2.   If your answer was 2, you're Bold with some work needed to boost you...

First, let me say that you do not need to explain anything to anyone, if you are a "Jesus Freak," then that's what you are! I mean you wouldn't mind being a "freak" for someone of the opposite sex that you are attracted to now, would you? (Be Honest and Keep it REAL!) Your Christianity should not be in question by anyone. There is no need to justify the "type" of Christian you are. All that matters is you are one and you belong to Him. After all, "we live life on levels and arrive in stages, and each level brings us to a new revelation and relationship with our God" (Nugget from Pastor A. R. Bernard).

If you answered yes to #3 and/or #4, first, you need to ask yourself, "why am I not comfortable answering this question?" Something made you choose to say yes to Christ in the first place, so what is the apprehension about you even wanting to talk about Him? Now if you had an experience like mine, I can understand why. However, if you are experiencing or have experienced something else that makes you want to just avoid Him, there may be a chance you do not have a connection with Him. If that is the case, it's okay because He is always available to connect with you. In fact, He wants to! I would also recommend reading the book of John in the Bible to help you build that connection with Him. This will help you to know Him on an intimate level and make Him real to you again. It will also help remind you of why you chose to accept Him in the beginning.

For those of you that answered "yes" to #4, the first course of action is to ask for His forgiveness of your denial of Him. As I stated earlier in the chapter, the scripture in Matthew 10:33 tells us that when we deny Him, He will deny us. I can assure you that He would never deny you, no matter what you do because He readily forgives. Knowing that nothing would make you deny Him, my next question is, who hurt you and made you believe He was not for you? Sometimes we allow the thoughts, opinions, and words of others make us believe God isn't for us and that isn't true. Get to know Him for yourself and not just to know Him but learn who He is to you on a personal level. Once you do that, you will find it next to impossible to deny Him ever again.

Unashamed Bold Faith

In today's world, bold faith in Jesus is becoming less and less favorable. Those of us who carry His name must not be ashamed to say His name, stand and speak up about the things that are contrary to Him and His original plan for life.

Today, many Christians feel pressured to live closed mouth and afraid of backlash and being labeled as a "hater", "weirdo", or "silly for following the white man's religion." I can say for myself that this notion of Christianity being a "white man's religion" is a clear indication that those who subscribe to that knowledge do not know the Father's true heart. They do not understand Him so they reject Him. We will never know what color Jesus/God is, all we know is His love, sacrifice, and forgiveness and that is really all that matters.

I don't have time to get into the origin of Christianity and where it came from and such; however, knowing a God enough to confess Him as Lord and Savior gave you enough courage to assure you that you needed Him. Having a working knowledge of Him plants a seed of faith and Boldness to carry you through this journey with Him.

Bold Faith in Action

I remember a time I was working at a job and I hated it after a while. I loved most of it, the people I worked with but the job made me upset and I wanted to leave. Just as fate would have it, the job was on the verge of closing and I had a choice of either leaving or staying to go with the new organization that would be taking over. I prayed about my decision of course first and I believe that God told me to leave.

I didn't have a guaranteed job at the time, no possible leads, just Bold Faith in God and the direction He was taking me in. My family thought I was crazy especially since I am a single mom of a then 4-year-old girl. How was I going to take care of and shelter her?

Surprisingly, that wasn't my concern; my concern was to listen to God because He had a plan. I chose at that moment to have bold faith and I had to constantly remind myself that He would supply all of our need according to His riches in glory and I just needed to trust Him. Faith is believing and doing, even when you do not see the floor in front of you but you keep walking because somehow the floor appears with each step.

BOLD FAITH TAKES BLIND TRUST

As I went through that season of choosing to be unemployed, God worked and was able to work so many miracles in and through me. Because I stepped out on faith despite what people said to me, I learned how to rely on Him and clearly hear His voice. I realized that once you quiet the voices around you, God's voice becomes louder, clearer and you are able to walk the path set out for you. Now, do not get me wrong, you can take advice from people and the Bible tells us to seek godly counsel. However, it should never supersede what you have heard God tell you. Trusting God is not doing what's comfortable and convenient. Trusting God is doing what is sometime crazy and uncomfortable but will build the confidence to trust even when you do not understand.

In the end, it worked out and I was able to build some character that ushered me into my next assignment. I ended up being able to take a position working with young people in schools, which is my passion. Had I lived with fear and under the voices of others, I would have missed my assignment. Trust God and have BOLD Faith. He will never fail you!

Bold Within
"For God has not given us a spirit of fear but of love, power and self-control" (1 Timothy 1:7).

I have a confession to make... I was never really the quiet type but I am shy at times. Yes, it's true. I don't like confrontation because I'd rather prefer things work itself out so I don't have to do anything. Wrong on some levels, I know but I am not the type to hurt people on purpose. Growing up, I was taught to be seen, not heard and my own opinions and thoughts were rarely expressed. I often kept my feelings to myself.

As I got older, I learned that I did indeed have a voice, a loud one at that and in recent years, I found that my voice is one that people actually want to hear. I would personally never consider myself a bold individual. I just tell the truth as I see fit and I add my opinion, usually solicited but in some cases unsolicited. Growing up, I had to understand a few things:

1. I was a child who was essentially abandoned.
2. A child must stay in a child's place, meaning if you had a vetoing opinion of those older than you, you kept it to yourself, dealt with it internally and moved on with life, with your voice stifled in the realm of "showing proper respect."
3. Everybody has a choice to make. Make the one that feels best for you.
Knowing these three essential things, when I became a teen/young adult, I lived my life out in that very way, quiet, shut down, and not knowing the power of my own voice.

By the time I turned 18 years old, I moved out of my mother's house and in with a relative who was willing to take me in, seeing as I had nowhere to go. Not only was that a grown move, it taught me how Bold I was, NOT to say the least. Since my childhood was a lot of me not expressing myself and speaking up for myself, living in this new environment was a shock to me because it truly showed me that I would have to learn to do away with how I grew up and learn my voice and how to use it. One of the biggest lessons I learned as an 18 year old, who was essentially living rent free, was that I didn't have a right to complain, but I was not happy with what was going on either. I realized that I had a right to speak up but I felt like I couldn't because I was not responsible for anything but myself. Well, it was not so much complaining as it was expressing how I felt about certain things and the way I was being treated. I felt often taken advantage of because of the state I was in; I was constantly reminded of how much I needed help.

As low it made me feel, I did not realize that I was being taught the biggest lesson that one can learn in life. It was through this experience that I learned that, finding your voice is the most powerful thing you will discover in life. That is why it is so important to hear a baby cry when they are born. It says, "I am here and I have something to say." I learned that there is a way to express myself without disrespecting others. Just like a baby, every voice is unique and is useful. Once I accepted that my voice was useful and deserved to be heard, ESPECIALLY when I know I had a lot to say, I started to speak and loudly!

Never Let Your Voice Be Silenced by Those Who Aren't willing to Listen!

Bold Confidence

The thing about being bold within is to have a certain level of confidence in yourself that if someone violates your personal values and morals, you have a license to tell them, "No, we are not doing this because this violates who I am and what I stand for" or "I don't appreciate that you did XYZ." Being able to stand up for yourself is not only bold, it takes Bold Confidence to do so. Let's be honest, we often shrink back from people because if you truly have a heart, you are thinking about that person's feelings or you just plain don't want to have the conversation.

Now, I am not saying to have confidence as arrogance, no but having that bold confidence is being able to say what you want, articulating what you don't want and holding people to that standard if they are

going to be in your space and yes, you have that right! I think it's so sad that people do not think they have a right to be Bold and Confident. Let me tell you, You Do! The other side of confidence is the assurance that you are enough and you have what it takes. Yes, I am talking to you! You are ENOUGH and You have what it takes to:
Succeed
Fulfill your dreams
Speak Up and Out
Live your life Freely
Fulfill the will of God for your life
You do not need ANYONE to tell you who you are. God told who you are and anything less than what God told you, which anyone might have spoken over you, is grounds for rejection!

Say it with me...
I am BOLD because it is ALREADY IN ME!

Living BRAVE when life challenges your Boldness...

Life will take you through challenges and trials often and that's the truth. The good news is when you have built your boldness on the foundation of Christ and you have become confident and sure of whom you are, life can shake you but it doesn't have to destroy you.

To live The B.R.A.V.E. Life, boldness is the first thing you must master when life comes from behind you and scares your faith right out of you. I am reminded of a time when I had my first job out of college and I had been there almost a year and I felt like I could not take it anymore. I was frustrated and was having issues with my supervisor. Being that it was my first job, I did not want to cause trouble or draw attention to myself but I knew I had to say something. I was terrified because, I am truly an adult at this point and I need to work to make money and take care of myself. I did not have anyone else to rely on but myself.

At work, I could feel tension and I sensed that I was on the verge of being fired. One night, I just got down on my knees and I asked and prayed to God to help me make the boldest choice of my life. Not knowing how it would end up, I was willing to take that risk.

The next day, when I went into work, having prayed up and gotten my "Godfidence," I spoke to my supervisors and I expressed my concerns and even pointed out where I was struggling. Even though that may not have been the smartest move, I was bold and took a risk in telling my truth and standing up for what I felt I needed to express on my terms. I ended up resigning from that position and took a job that catered more to my own needs and creativity. I would not have done that had I not been bold and took courage. If I can do it, You can Too!

Be willing to take risks.

When living the B.R.A.V.E. Life, living bold is being able to take risks in situations that may not be favorable to you and to those closest to you, especially when you are facing challenging moments such as losing your home and having to ask people to live with them. You cannot allow your pride to get in the way of what you need. You have to be willing to hear "NO" and be prepared to have plan A, B, and C ready to implement.

You have to be willing to put yourself out there and get help that you may not normally dream of getting because you are used to a certain way of living and being. Being bold and living the B.R.A.V.E. Life is definitely living outside of the box and making your decisions out the box too. When it comes to your faith, it definitely will mean you having to risk the talk, stares, and opinions of others and what they "think" God wants you to do. You have to ask yourself, "Am I willing to risk getting judged by those I love to live Bold in The B.R.A.V.E. Life"?

The truth is, everyone is not going to understand *what* you are doing and *why* and in most cases, you will not have an explanation to give them. The essence of being Bold and choosing to live the B.R.A.V.E. is to do it without apology, doing what you feel, being led by God and wanting to be bold enough to honor yourself in every capacity of the process.

When you find yourself in a challenging situation where you are shrinking back and becoming afraid because you are unsure of the next move, you know that your boldness is under attack. I am going to tell you something, in that very moment, tell yourself:

"I am Bold Enough to get through this because my Faith anchors me, God covers me, and I am His."

I want to leave you with this:

3 Bold Tools to use when life attacks your faith and confidence
1. Change your perspective of what is going on. Know that may be hard but if you remember that what you are facing is teaching you a lesson, it will help you to see your strength and build the character of boldness on the inside of you.

2. Remember your voice! When you are going through a tough and/or challenging moment, you will want to crawl in a hole and retreat. This is the time to step out, speak up, and say exactly what you want and need.

3. Use your confidence with your Boldness. It is already in you!

Boldness in the B.R.A.V.E. Life
Thoughts and Reflective Questions to Consider...
1. What are you going to do to start or continue walking in your Bold Faith?

_____

_____

_____

_____

_____

_____

2. What is holding you back?

_____

_____

_____

_____

_____

_____

_____

_____

_____

Your BRAVE Thoughts...
Use the following pages to write your thoughts about the chapter and how you are going to live BOLD in your Life!

_____

_____

_____

_____

_____

_____

_____

_____

_____

_____

_____

_____

_____

_____
_____
_____
_____
_____
_____
_____
_____
_____
_____
_____
_____
_____
_____
_____
_____
_____
_____
_____
_____
_____
_____
_____
_____
_____
_____
_____

BRAVE BONUS

Bold Faith Confession

Do you know Christ personally and have a foundation in Him? If you have never confessed Jesus and you want to start building Bold Faith, say this prayer with me:

Father God in the Name of Jesus, I am a sinner, who desires to be saved by your loving grace. I confess and recognize that I have sinned against you. I repent right now of all that I have done, said, or thought, which was not pleasing to you. I ask that you forgive me and receive me as your child. I believe that you are the one true Son of God, you came to earth to die for me and you rose again on the third day and you will come back for me. I accept you as my Lord and Savior. I will walk with you because your word said that you would be with me even unto the ends of the earth. Thank You for hearing this prayer. In Jesus' Name, I pray. Amen.

For the new Bold Faith walkers, it will take time to build that boldness but you can start by reading the book of John to build that relationship with your heavenly Father. Second, read Joshua 1:7-9 to build the character of Boldness and courage within you!

BOLD Declaration

I am not afraid of what I can't   see.

I walk anyway because He walks beside me.

I am not unsure of what I was purposed to do;

He gives me the blueprint for my life to walk in the Boldness that's new.

2

BE Resilient

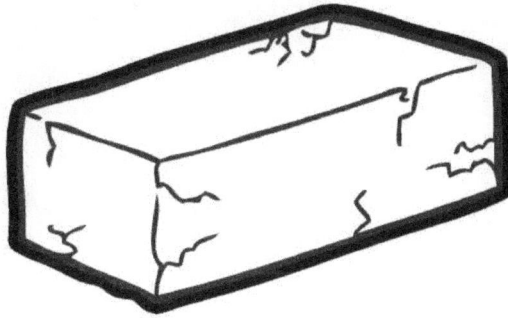

"The ability to recoil or spring back into shape after bending, stretching, or being compressed. Having the capacity to recover or withstand quickly."

Poem
Rubber-band
Pulled and pushed to and fro
struggling and wondering which way to go.
I can't see my way,
this way I can't stay
My eyes are burning
my heart is yearning for something different,
when will I see the change?
Back and forth
The test remains, somehow I sustain
like a Rubber-Band

Resilient in the Midst of Storms
"Always have a relentless drive for progress" (Pastor AR Bernard)

Never did I dream that I would be a hurdle jumper. No, I have never run track but my life has been one hurdle jump after another. When I was born, the doctor told my mom that I would never walk because I had *spina bifida*. It's a neural tube defect that affects the bladder control and bowel movements of an individual. In fact, most people with spina bifida are in wheelchairs, have shunts (a tube that runs from the brain to release fluid), they are unable to care for themselves, and have limited mobility. Looking at me, you would never know anything was wrong, that is a blessing from God. So from day one, that was the first hurdle to jump over.

The cards of life I was dealt, sometimes I felt was stacked against me. Being born with such an illness was not so challenging until I started going to school. When I entered into elementary school, I was "labeled." I lived approximately five blocks from school and from elementary school to junior high school, I had to take the school bus, or as some students "affectionately" called it "the cheese bus." Each day, I left my class a half hour early to meet "the cheese bus" and everyday every 2 hours, I was picked up by an aide to take me to the bathroom to catheterize myself. This was because, with the spina bifida condition, the muscles that push out the urine was not strong enough to do so, so I have to self-cath every two hours.

Most of the kids wondered why I needed someone to take me to the bathroom and I could not explain to them—one, because they would never understand and two, I was so embarrassed to tell them that I wore pampers due to my bladder problem, over which I had no control. I was mortified when I got to intermediate school and all the girls wore those tight jeans and I wore jeans that were loose so as not to show the "pamper butt" I had. I often thought to myself, "God must not really like me that much. If He did, why am I not normal like everyone else? I just want to be like everyone else."

That hurdle I had to jump taught me that being different was something I would have to get used to. As you also would imagine, I was teased a lot. Questions were often asked and I would want to shrink and disappear into the air. As I got older, my lesson in resiliency intensified. Being a product of the foster care system, homelessness, a victim of rape, and almost committing suicide at the age of 19, being resilient became a part of who I am. During those trying moments, I soon discovered that there was a reason for it all.

When my birth mom was not able to take care of me and I was adopted, I felt abandoned but then I realized that I was special because someone took the time to take care of me and bring me into their family as their own.

When I was put out of my adopted mother's house and was homeless, I felt rejected once again. The fact that I had no choice but to go live with a man I knew, who ended up raping me and taking advantage of me, I felt like this is better than being on the streets. I did not want to be riding the trains every night but there were nights when I would be walking the streets of the Bronx 2am and 3am because I did not want to encounter the man who was raping me. I did not know at the time how I would get out, but I was determined to stick with it because deep inside, I knew this was not for me.

The moment I decided I would take my own life, I was faced with two options. Either I would end it all and that would be it for me or I could fight through what I was going through and just believe things would change eventually. In the end, I had the most powerful spiritual encounter and at this point in my life, the choice was made for me and I was given the strength to fight through it because, there was more of life for me to live and I would not be in that place forever.

Resilience within anchored in Faith

How many times have we asked the question, "Why Me?" A dozen million times, right? Well, have you ever asked yourself, "Why Not Me?" Let me explain something to you, whenever a storm enters into your life (and there will be storms, so accept it!), you have a few choices to make. You can either succumb to the storms or let them drown you and you get washed away or you can put your gear on and get through it so you can see the sun shining again in your life.

Everyone goes through things, it's how you handle it that makes a difference and allows you to pursue life with resilience.

I am going to be completely honest; in order to truly pursue your life with strength and resilience when facing storms, you need

God—and He is there with you in the midst of the storms. The book of life, the Bible tells us,

"When the enemy comes in like a flood, the Spirit of the Lord will lift up a standard against him. The Redeemer will come to Zion" (Isaiah 59:19-20).

This scripture alone has anchored my life and has given me everything I need to pursue my goals through whatever comes my way. The scripture is descriptive in talking about how the enemy comes in like a flood. Flood, in meaning, is to have something **"arrive in overwhelming amounts or quantities" (V).** In understanding the magnitude in which how life can overtake you, we can all conclude that the adversary of our lives can sometimes come in such an overwhelming way that we feel as though we do not have the capacity to handle it. On the contrary, God Himself, being the amazing God that He is, steps in and raises His standard, which is His word, His way of life, the way He intended for us to live. God brings that to the forefront of the storm that is intended to overtake us, and anything that does not line up with that standard and way of life, it has to go!

To face the enemy of your life, you must pursue him with armor and God is that armor. Along with that, you must have the ability to speak to the storms that come into your life with Boldness. Jesus teaches that in Mark:

35 That day when evening came, he said to his disciples, "Let us go over to the other side."36Leaving the crowd behind, they took him along, just as he was, in the boat. There were also other boats with him.37<u>A furious squall came up, and the waves broke over the boat, so that it was nearly swamped.</u>38 Jesus was in the stern, sleeping on a cushion. The disciples woke him and said to him, <u>"Teacher, don't you care if we drown?"</u> 39 He got up, rebuked the wind and said to the waves, <u>"Quiet! Be still! "Then the wind died down and it was completely calm. 40 He said to his disciples, "Why are you so afraid? Do you still have no faith?"</u> (Mark 4:35-41).

Isn't that like life? I mean, let's look at this for a second. Our lives can be going decent and then suddenly you see "clouds" brewing in the form of bills coming and you having not enough income to address them. Then suddenly you start having problems at work and you are on the brink of losing your job. Then you lose your

THE BRAVE LIFE

job and your income is decreasing and the bills continue to come. You start to panic; you know you need to keep a roof over your head and your children's head and you shout to God, "Don't you CARE?!" In that very moment, Jesus is quiet, you don't hear Him move, shuffle or anything! The storm begins to rage, you start to get notices of eviction and you are wondering if God really cares about you.

This is where resilience comes in and pursuing life takes full shape. Are you going to wag your finger at God and blame Him or will you have Faith to believe that there is something waiting in the winds to help you? It is during the storm that God is teaching you how to trust Him without reacting to what is going on around you? Instead of constantly focusing on what the storm is doing, speak to it and tell it to do what you desire for it to do. We cannot really stop the storm but we can change the directions of the winds and put on the gear to protect us while going through. When Jesus got up, all He did was say "Quiet and Be Still." I tend to think that Jesus was not really speaking to the storm, He was speaking to His disciples and their spirits who did not trust that He could take care of them. It is evident because afterward, He said, "Why are you so afraid? Do you STILL have faith?" In order to pursue life in the midst of the storms, you must STILL have faith. You must be willing to hold onto the faith that the enemy is trying to shake off your hands in the flood he's brought against you.

You have the power to speak to the storms in your life and your spirit and say, "Quiet and Be Still!" I was having a conversation with my cousin and I told her a striking fact that, in order to "Be Still," you must understand what that truly means. To "Be" means to "exist, occur and take place." To be "still" is "deep silence and calm." In essence, when the Word tells us to "Be Still," it literally means to exist in silence and calm. Sometimes, that doesn't mean to not "do" anything while in a storm, it means to be calm. In whatever you are going through, you have the ability to tell yourself, your spirit to exist in calmness.

I can admit that it is difficult to do it but I want you to think about what happens when someone is screaming and yelling in your face. Do you yell and scream at them at the same level? NO, you do not match their intensity. You speak calmly and without aggression and at some point, that person will match your calm and stillness.

This is the same approach to use in the midst of the storm and how you can pursue resilience in your storms of life.

Approach them:

1. **Anchored in God and His word**
2. **With stillness, calm, and without intense reaction**
3. **With strategy and a plan of action**

Living BRAVE when Life challenges your Resilience

This element of the BRAVE Life is the anchor of this lifestyle. To be resilient, you must be willing to be tossed to and fro but have the ability to bounce back. When you accept that you will be faced with things wherein you may not see your way out of immediately, you will have difficulty dealing with them, or you will have to make decisions that will be challenging. In all, you must make the choice to remain and stay the course till the end.

Be willing to grow your Strength and Get Focused

The Bible says in James 1:3,

"Dear brothers and sisters, when troubles come your way, consider it an opportunity for great joy. For you know that when your faith is tested, your endurance has a chance to grow. So let it grow, for when your endurance is fully developed, you will be perfect and complete, needing nothing."

Being resilient and living the BRAVE life is letting your storms and challenges make you strong. It's accepting what is happening, which may seem negative at the time, and allowing it to be an opportunity for you to learn the lesson attached to it and make you stronger. It's like going to the gym for the first time, when you first start, it makes you want to quit because it gets painful, your body isn't used to it and you are sore all over. Then once you see the results of it, you develop a plan that works for you, and once you start working that plan, it gets better and better, easier and easier and then eventually, you have changed for the better and you can see what the work has produced in you.

Being resilient allows you to develop the thick skin you need to overcome every obstacle. It challenges you to engage in the change that you wish to see in yourself and experience the results of the work you put in.

I want to leave you with this:

3 Resilient Tools to use when life challenges attacks your Faith:

1.   **Accept the storms and let them have their work.** They are your resistance to help you build the muscle of resilience.

2.   **Learn the art of "Be Still." Exist Calmly.**

3.   **Make the most of every challenge** and turn your negative experience into an opportunity to anchor yourself and keep moving forward.

Let resilience be a muscle in your life that you work when the life storms of resistance come your way!

Resilience in the B.R.A.V.E. Life
Thoughts and Reflective Questions to Consider...
1. In your experiences, the negative ones, how do you usually handle them?

_____

_____

_____

_____

2. What in your life can you say is now building resilience in your life?

_____

_____

_____

_____

_____

_____

Your BRAVE Thoughts
Use the following pages to write your thoughts about the chapter and how you are going to be **Resilient** in your Life!

_____

_____

_____

_____

_____

_____

_____

_____

_____

_____

_____

_____

_____

_____

_____

_____

_____

_____
_____
_____
_____
_____
_____
_____
_____
_____
_____
_____
_____

RESILIENT Declaration

I can make it through every storm.
I am never on my own.
He walks beside me.
His Word anchors me.
I have a purpose to fulfill.
I was created to do His will.
Nothing will EVER stop me!

3

BE Authentic

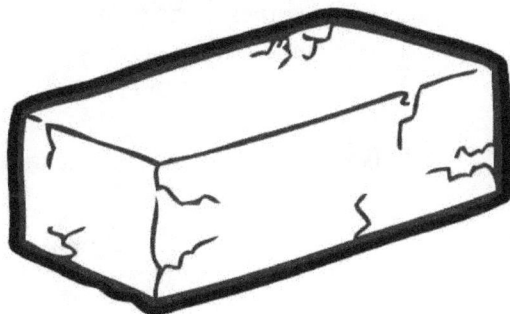

"An undisputed origin; genuine. Made or done in a way that faithfully resembles the original."

Poem
The Me I LOVE to be

Every time I look in the mirror,
she stares,
she smiles
her dark nappy hair, so hard to tame.
Her curves of size 12 and 14
often called a "plain Jane"...
I Love Her

She feels good to me.

I walk past the mirror,
I see her light,
she shines so bright,
He is within her
Her speech is pure,

She is so real, she has battle scars
and wounds
She knows she's a winner
She will Not lose,

She feels Good to me

She is Me
Chocolate Brown Girl
loving every curve
Hanging on every word she speaks
I Love The Me I see
The Me, I Love to Be!

Authentic Within
"For you created my inmost being; you knit me together in my mother's womb."

Everybody wants to be somebody...even if it's the body they do not have residence of. They want some "other" body, they want to "be" some "other" body, because their somebody is not like the "other" somebody. Have you ever felt like someone was living the life you were supposed to have so you took it upon yourself to live like that person but it didn't work out too well for you? NO? It's just me? Okay...
Well, let me tell you what happened with me...

I grew up as a foster child. My birth mom was a drug addict, I didn't know my birth father (still don't) and at the age of 6, I went into foster care. You already know I was born with a disability, so I had every bad thing to happen to me before I was 10 years old! What kind of life is that? I often thought, "God must have really had it out for me."

One day I was watching TV, I had to be about 7/8 and there were these little girls. I don't remember the show, but they were little white girls and I thought, "Man, white people have it a lot better than black people. Their hair is longer, they are prettier, have nice houses, I want that." Yep, that's what I said at 7/8. I used to put a shirt over my head and swing it like it was my hair (Don't act like you didn't do it either!). I thought being white, with long hair, was the life I got cheated out of. For years, I struggled with being who I was, a beautiful chocolate brown girl.

When I became a teenager, I began to realize that maybe it was not so bad to be black. I started to like myself more and after my mom and sister told me how amazing it was to be black, I started to accept myself until I realized there was a shade scale. The darker you were, the less attractive you were. The lighter you were, the more attractive you were. So now, I had gotten over wanting to be white, now I am too dark, what gives?! One day, I was hanging out with a friend and she and I went to Burger King. There were a group of guys in there so, of course, we had to be a little extra. There had to be at least 5 of them, and all 5 wanted my friend and not me; she was light skinned. I remember feeling like, there must be something wrong with me and from that day, I began to learn to study people, their behavior, what made them attractive because if I could not change my skin color, I could change my behavior to be like those that were liked and accepted. The problem with that is, it was not me, but my desperation to be liked and loved was so real that I didn't care; I wanted to be somebody...somebody other than *me*.

Un-Authentic in Relationships
Authenticity in Family
My family had an impeccable way of showing me the mirror of myself. I grew up around some very powerful and strong women and all of them were unapologetic about telling the truth. My mother being the matriarch that she is had a very strong way of telling you how she felt with no apologies. You just sucked it up and took it, no matter how it came to you. I remember distinctively one day I had just come home from school and I was talking to her about something. She turned around very curtly and said, "You are black Takima, black."

At first, I was confused as to why she was saying this but then it dawned on me that the way I spoke must have made her feel as though I was trying to be someone I wasn't. In other words, I must have been talking "white" (which is a term I truly do not understand). Although this was something I had heard before, I took that statement to heart because I looked at the way I was speaking and deep down inside, I felt I was speaking the way I knew how, but possibly it was not the way I was supposed to speak. From that day on, I practiced speaking differently or more "black" but it just did not work.

As time went on, I realized that when you are who you are, many people will not always get you or your way of being and that is okay. As long as you are true to *you*, that is what matters. My mother wasn't wrong in what she said to me, it was up to me to accept what she said and live that out, but then I had to ask myself the honest question of,

"Is this really who I am authentically"?

Authenticity in Friendships
The friendships I have acquired and built in my life has become the crux of who I am at the core. My friends, my core group of friends

are the people that I have close to me and essentially look up to, mainly because they are mostly older than me and I am the "little sister." The struggle though, being the youngest in your group of friends, is that sometimes you can get caught up in trying to "keep up." I totally fell into that trap. Most of my friends were in school and were on a very focused path. I, on the other hand, was trying to figure out life and often times found myself stumbling through my own life.

When they started getting married and having children, I started to feel so left out. I felt like my life was just dumb (for a lack of better words) and that I was not significant enough.

So in order to keep up, I tried to "find" my purpose in following in their footsteps. They all had degrees and were in school. I did community service and then went to school. I remember one particular day, I was in church. One of my friends had texted me she was pregnant and this was the second friend to tell me she was pregnant! I began to feel like, "Dang, can I graduate first and then you all can have kids." I felt like I could never be on their "level."

At the time, the church I was attending, the pastor began to always talk to me about being authentic and stop trying to please people. I was continuously frustrated because hearing the same word over and over made me feel like I was not changing and that there was something wrong with me.

It wasn't until one of the elders of the church said to me "Takima, you are not your friends. You will never be like them. Your path is different and your life will not look like theirs." That was a tough pill to swallow but it was the truth. I was trying so hard to keep up with them that I was missing out on the life God had specifically designed for me.

When I graduated, started working and then eventually had my daughter (minus the husband), it hit me. It was my daughter's first birthday and they all came to celebrate with us. When the party was done, they left, in their cars with their husbands and children. I felt so sad and just broken. I pushed my baby girl and all of her gifts back to my brother's house. I was alone, a single woman with a baby. I wanted the husband, the family, the car and I didn't. It wasn't until then, that I realized I was trying to be like them and although I believe God has a husband and greater life planned for me, that was not my reality at that time and in that moment, it made me feel inadequate and just a failure at life. What I started to realize though, this is what made me different and being different is what makes me truly authentic.

Your Reflection is Your Truth

When you look in the mirror, what does it tell you? Go with me to the book of James, chapter 1 vs 23-25:

Anyone who listens to the word but does not do what it says is like someone who looks at his face in a mirror and, after looking at himself, goes away and immediately forgets what he looks like. But whoever looks intently into the perfect law that gives freedom, and continues in it—not forgetting what they have heard, but doing it—they will be blessed in what they do.

I want to highlight the part that says, "ANYONE who LISTENS to the word but does NOT do what it says is like someone who LOOKS at HIS FACE IN A MIRROR AND AFTER LOOKING AT HIMSELF, goes away and IMMEDIATELY FORGETS what He looks like.

When you, we, I read the word of God, it says that we are Fearfully and Wonderfully made, it says that We CAN DO ALL THINGS Through CHRIST who gives us strength. It says we are MADE in HIS image and HIS Likeness.

Now, you may not even be a Christian or saved but I am going to tell you there is a God who has made you so incredible that there is NEVER a need to feel inferior to ANYONE! If you are saved, you are like this man described in James. You KNOW the God that created you! YOU KNOW the God that has placed a purpose in your heart, WHY on earth would you try to be like someone else?

Who Told YOU, You were not enough?

I had to ask myself that question many times. To be authentic and true to yourself, you must look at the deepest parts of you and your story. You must look deep into the ones you don't like to tell and find the root of the story of "who told you, you were not enough?" and said that "If you are like that, you will be great." Someone gave you new information and it has taken root in you and now it is growing into this experience that you call life and you are living unauthentic because someone TOLD you, You were not enough!

You need to CUT IT! Cut That Root OUT!

Who changed your mind about who God said you are?

You are quiet, who told you that powerful people are the loud ones? Do you know that silent leaders have the most power? Who told you that you have to have long hair to be perceived as beautiful? Yes, the Bible says your hair is your crown but the Bible also says a woman's beauty is not in what she wears, or her jewelry but a quiet and gentle spirit. If you are kind and warm, you are Beautiful!

Every time I speak now, I love every word that comes out of my mouth and how I express myself. It is unique to me and to the very person God designed me to be.

Who are you pretending to be?

Have you let someone change your makeup and your authentic way of being? As I said before, my mother was just expressing what she thought I was doing that was not real but when I found that it was who I am, I continued to be that person. Do Not let what others think or say about you change how you present yourself to the world! People may not understand it but the most important thing for you to do and remember is that if it feels comfortable for you, then it is You! Authentically!

Your voice is the most powerful tool you have and when you see that people are trying to silence it or change its sound, that is when you have to look deep within and hold onto it that much tighter. Don't let ANYONE change the sound of your voice! There is a reason there are various sounds and tones on instruments. No tone and sound is the same and neither are you! Own your voice, Your Sound and Your Tone!

In the same vein, within friendships and even relationships, you must be true to who you are and the life God intended you to live. Are you finding yourself comparing your life to your friends? Are you trying to keep up with them and finding yourself falling further behind? Let me tell you right now, STOP IT!

Your life is different from theirs for a reason. Honestly think about it, if you and your friends ALL had the same life, how can you help, inspire, encourage or strengthen one another? You all would be living the SAME life. How boring and unfulfilled is that? It's okay to have similarities but following the same path will not do anything to edify each other.

You are called out for a reason, you have a different lifestyle for a reason, and you MUST be authentic for a reason! Don't you know that you have a call on your life that is so specific that your friends cannot reach those you are called to? If you tried or are trying to be like them, you are not only being unauthentic but you are making those who are waiting on you miss out on their blessing!

Consider this...

Now if the foot should say, "Because I am not a hand, I do not belong to the body," it would not for that reason stop being part of the body. And if the ear should say, "Because I am not an eye, I do not belong to the body," it would not for that reason stop being part of the body. If the whole body were an eye, where would the sense of hearing be? If the whole body were an ear, where would the sense of smell be? But in fact God has placed the parts in the body, every one of them, just as he wanted them to be. If they were all one part, where would the body be? As it is, there are many parts, but one body ~ 1 Corinthians 12:15-20

**Living BRAVE When life Challenges your Authenticity –
Authentic in Business**
(This One is a BRAVE BONUS)

Who told you, you have to sell your products or services like the person that is making millions of dollars? Maybe you are not meant to make millions of dollars and your approach to those who are called to meet or patronize you are not attracted to being "sold" but "told" about who you are and what you offer. I am learning this now as I am building this platform that God has given to me. I tried following a blueprint, watching what other people do, how they do it and putting my own spin on it and that is exactly what I ended up doing, spinning—spinning my wheels and not making progress. I was not being authentic.

There is NOTHING NEW but You Are!

The truth of the matter is there is nothing new under the sun. Everything that is being done has been done, 20 million times over. Although you are new to this earth, anything you do isn't. So why not be who you are and let the world see you for just that? I mean let's face it, you can try to be "original" but honestly, that is a slim to none gesture.

Your authenticity is unique to you, just like with your fingerprint, it's distinct to you, OWN IT.

I am going to leave you with this:
3 Authentic Tools to use when your authenticity is challenged
PLUS 2 Bonus tools!
1.   **Know who you are from within.** Being authentic starts with you. Some people are ashamed of who they are, especially if they have a bad past. They want to forget who they used to be and "recreate" themselves.

2.   You cannot do that, sorry! The only thing you can do is change the way you do things and make choices that are conducive to where you are trying to go. Your past is something that happened to you but I challenge you to look at it as a happening for you. Your authenticity is wrapped in your experiences.

3.   **Learn the ART of loving your own unique set of abilities and gifts.** Too often we are focused on what others do, how they are, how they act, we actually subconsciously imitate them. The reason we do this is because we do not know or haven't tapped into the great person we are yet to become. We often think because we see others advancing, being recognized, and in relationships (come on, let's be honest), we have to change something within us to obtain that. The truth is, we don't have to. The validity of our own personality, gifts and talents are ENOUGH! I want you to recognize and realize YOU ARE ENOUGH!
        Take the time to get to know YOU! The foundation of authenticity is knowing yourself In and Out. Think about when you are getting to know someone, what do you do? You take time to

talk to them, you go out with them and you learn information about their life. You find out what they like, what they don't like, what ticks them off, what makes them smile, what makes them sad, right? Do you know that about *you*? Do you know what makes you get out of the bed in the AM? If you don't, I suggest spending some quality time with you. Write in a journal daily and write out your thoughts for the day. You will learn quite a lot about yourself and as you do, you will discover you will want to be no one else.

* Be an innovator! Most people who are authentic are innovators. They are known to step outside of the box and do things differently from how everyone else is doing it. Even if it's the same thing, it's never the same way. Think of ways to put a spin on the market, your product, service, social media, #BLACKGIRLMAGIC (Create You Own Hashtag or Make it Better). You CAN DO THAT! You just have to believe you are dope enough to do it.

* Always, always Be Yourself! No matter what anyone says about you, what you're doing, how you speak, Always Be Yourself! You are the ONLY ONE created by God in this world, and that makes you an original. Now just add your Authentic touch!

You Are the ONLY One there is in the world; Make it Count Abundantly

Authenticity in the B.R.A.V.E. Life
BRAVE Thoughts and Reflective Questions to Consider......
1. What makes you authentic?

_____
_____
_____
_____
_____
_____
_____

_____

2. When was the time or is it now where you have not been or are not authentic? How can you change that? List your ways below.

_____
_____
_____
_____
_____
_____
_____
_____
_____

Your BRAVE Thoughts
Use the following pages to write your thoughts about the chapter and how you are going to live **Authentic** in your Life!

_____
_____
_____
_____
_____
_____
_____
_____
_____
_____
_____

_____

_____

AUTHENTIC Declaration
There is NO ONE in this world better than ME!
God created me — Great, Good, Authentically Designed.
I carry His DNA with me.
There is NO ONE that can do what I do.
I have a unique Heart and Spirit, that's True.
There are times I fall short, and that's okay.
I will do what I do Always in the best possible way.
I am not afraid of copycats and replicas;
I let them shine Just Because
They are them, and I am *Me*.
I do what NO ONE Can Do
AUTHENTICALLY!

4

BE Victorious

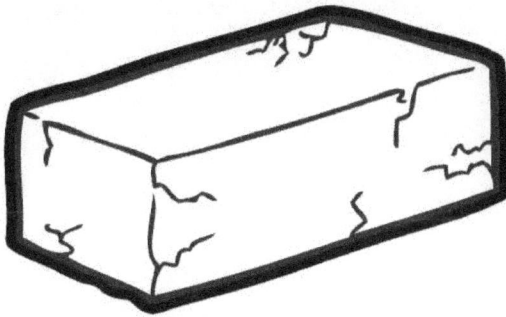

"A success or superior position achieved against any opponent, opposition, difficulty."

*But thank God! He gives us Victory over sin and death through our Lord Jesus Christ" - **1 Corinthians 15:5-7***

Poem
What is that I See?
Over the horizon through the thick of the clouds of turmoil and complacency.
I think it's Victory...
When the world turns against me and there is pain,
the whispers of despair pour down like rain,
I yearn for Victory.
Life passes by in the blink of an eye and the flooding of words and "I'm sorries" overflow
Yeah, I smell Victory.
She comes so subtle but with force, not missing a beat, she takes over the smallest feat.
Her name is Victory!
Nothing stands in her way
She makes her presence known and her residence in Me is here to Stay!

Victory over circumstances
"Christ causes us to triumph."

I have to say I am somewhat pensive and excited to write this chapter. My life wasn't victorious at all but the moment I decided that I wanted victory, that's when I started to see it—kind of like the saying that goes, "when the student is ready, the teacher will appear." How many of you "feel" victorious? If you said, "I do," congrats! Because most of us do not feel victorious because of what we might have gone through, experienced, or had to endure, and there was nothing victorious about it. What I found out, however, later in life is that there are small victories that happen in your life that get ignored and then the big ones come eventually and they get recognized and celebrated instantly! Why is that? Why aren't the small ones celebrated like the big ones?

Do you realize that when you celebrate your small wins, those are the doors that open to the bigger ones? But you didn't think that, did you? Let me make it plainer, I will tell you a story. When my daughter was about 5 months old, we were living with my brother in his one bedroom apartment in The Bronx. He was so gracious enough to let us live there and at the time, I had nowhere else to go. In the process, I was struggling with postpartum depression and I was frustrated with having to go from having my own apartment to having to live in my brother's living room with my infant. Needless to say, I was humiliated. I was embarrassed and I felt like this is not the life I wanted, especially with a child. I felt less than victorious and did not see any victory in my life at all.

Five months into living with my brother, I took it upon myself and moved out (against God's direction, of course). I moved into a basement studio apartment and I felt like "this is better for me because this is MY PLACE." To make a long story short, I had to end up moving right back to my brother's house because the apartment was not in good condition as I had thought and God did not tell me to leave my brother's house. So I went back and for two years, I lived with my brother. I felt even more frustrated, embarrassed, and non-victorious. I thought God was punishing me for a whole host of reasons and I could not understand why He would not let me leave. Why can't I be independent?! What I realize now is that God was showing me how to celebrate the small victories in my life because when I did that, I would have room to celebrate the larger ones.

During that year of being with my brother, I began to look at all the things that I experienced and how God truly had been there the whole time and that I did have victories to celebrate. I was so consumed with the fact that I was in my brother's living room, I was out of work (I had gotten 'let go' from my job 2 months into living with him), I started a master's program and failed a class my first semester, I was extremely depressed (suffered with postpartum and had to go through therapy), I stopped going to church (I lost my faith in God), and I just felt like my life was headed nowhere.

One day, right before the shift happened, God opened my eyes and allowed the scales to fall off. I was at my best friend's house and I was feeling so defeated, I cried and just let out how I was feeling about my life and I could not understand what I did so wrong to be going through such an awful life. As I cried and prayed, God showed me my year. Living with my brother for that year and a half, I learned how to take care of myself. I acknowledged how I felt about the transition of being a mother, the frustrations that surround that transition and He gave me the strength to get help, **(VICTORY)**.

I learned how to begin to love my baby girl by seeing in her all the things I desired to see as a little girl myself. I wasn't complete in loving her but I was finally learning how to **(VICTORY)**. I stepped out in faith and did freelance work, something I had never done before and I was successful. I learned some areas in my life I needed to work on and I am continuing to this day to get better with it **(VICTORY)**. I challenged myself in starting my masters. It was a huge accomplishment in me taking that step WITH a child. I am still in the process of completing my thesis, but I did complete and pass all of my coursework **(VICTORY)**. I began to rebuild the relationship with my birth mother after God was able to show me all the hurt, anger, and unforgiveness I had held in my heart against her **(VICTORY)**.

When God showed me all these things, I wept even more. Through it all, I had not given up. I didn't give up on myself, my life, on being a mom, and the dreams God placed on the inside of me. He gave me victory through it all and I was able to go forward in the next phase.

After that day, I was able to get an apartment with NO paystubs. They accepted my freelance work and the child support money I was getting (who does that? God does). Two months later, I was hired as an executive assistant at a non-for-profit organization, (I have never had that position before, and again God came through). I started my master's program again and passed every class! When that happened, I realized that when I acknowledged the smaller victories, then the larger victories were able to manifest.

The Jonah experience

Many times during this season of my life, I felt like I was having a "Jonah Experience." I knew God had told me to do certain things but because I was convinced that my way was better, I took it upon myself and did what I felt I should do. When I left my brother's house and had to go right back, that experience was like when God told Jonah to go to Nineveh and he decided he was going to go to Tarshish instead. Jonah 1:1-11,

The word of the Lord came to Jonah son of Amittai: "Go to the great city of Nineveh and preach against it, because its wickedness has come up before me." But Jonah ran away from the Lord and headed for Tarshish. He went down to Joppa, where he found a ship bound for that port. After paying the fare, he went aboard and sailed for Tarshish to flee from the Lord.

Then the Lord sent a great wind on the sea, and such a violent storm arose that the ship threatened to break up. All the sailors were afraid and each cried out to his own god. And they threw the cargo into the sea to lighten the ship.

But Jonah had gone below deck, where he lay down and fell into a deep sleep. The captain went to him and said, "How can you sleep? Get up and call on your god! Maybe he will take notice of us so that we will not perish."

Then the sailors said to each other, "Come, let us cast lots to find out who is responsible for this calamity." They cast lots and the lot fell on Jonah. So they asked him, "Tell us, who is responsible for making all this trouble for us?

What kind of work do you do? Where do you come from? What is your country? From what people are you?"

He answered, "I am a Hebrew and I worship the Lord, the God of

heaven, who made the sea and the dry land."
This terrified them and they asked, "What have you done?" (They knew he was running away from the Lord, because he had already told them so.)
The sea was getting rougher and rougher. So they asked him, "What should we do to you to make the sea calm down for us?"

You as the Jonah in your life

There is a time in all of our lives where we are Jonah. We know we are called and chosen to do something and instead of going in the direction that God is directing us, we go the complete opposite way. Many times, it is because we are fearful of what we will encounter. When we think of Jonah, the place God intended for him to go was a place where the people were rebellious against God. Jonah didn't believe that they would listen to him and he was afraid of what they would say and do to him delivering such a brash message.

For you, it may be the same thing. God has called you to speak a word to someone who may not be willing to hear it but it doesn't change the fact that He called YOU to deliver it. The longer you hold that message, you are holding back the victory to be experienced in not only that person or those people's lives but also, you are blocking the victory you are supposed to experience in your OWN life. There is always victory in God and whether you see it or not, God will make sure that You Experience it, including those assigned to you!

You CANNOT run from God!

Is there something that God has told you to do that you are running from? Let me tell you firsthand and from scripture, you CANNOT run from God. He will "find" you and you WILL do what He has called you to do. I know sometimes it can be intimidating and downright scary to do what God calls us to do. What you have to realize is that when God called you to preach, teach, sing, write, dance, or speak to a particular people or person, He has placed something in you so special that Only You can do it.

What I found in life, especially with having a call on your life, you will always face challenges. You will always encounter challenges that will test the validity of your faith but it is also what you will need to accomplish the task that you were called to complete. In order to truly experience victory in life, you have to be "proven by trials." Like I said earlier, you have to be willing and open to celebrate the smaller victories because those are the doors that open to the bigger ones you will experience. The first key and step is to stop running!

Are you willing to stop running and come out of the "whale"?

Living BRAVE when Life Challenges Victory

I know you may be wondering how the BRAVE life connects with the story of Jonah and living Victorious. The story of Jonah has everything to do with Victory and living The BRAVE Life. Remember what I told you about moving from my brother's house and having to come right back? That was the lowest point of my life because I felt like I was not making any progress. It was like I was in the belly of the fish.

What I didn't realize at the time was that God was working some things out in me that I would not have gotten had I stayed where I had gone running off to. I believe I would not have experienced the victories I did when I returned to where God had sent me.

You must be willing to persevere to gain the victory.

In order to experience victory in The BRAVE Life, you have to be willing to persevere. You have to be willing to climb those tough mountains and face those tough challenges when there is NO victory in sight. There will be moments when you are constantly surrounded by defeat, fear, and doubt. Your ability to see past that is what will carry you to the victory you desire to experience.

Think about when a soldier is at war. They are faced with death, blood, losing other soldiers that were once beside them but they do not stop fighting. They do not pack up their gear and leave because all they are facing is death. Living BRAVE means to stay the course, no matter how tough it gets. Things WILL DIE around you and even inside of you, but will you quit? Will you walk away when you have fought with everything you have and you feel like that there is nothing left?

Whatever it is, you must muster that faith that is stuffed deep down within you and use that to help you get over that last bridge. It won't be easy, I will tell you that. When I sat on my friend's couch that night and just fell apart, I wanted to give up, but if I had, I would have forfeited the victory that was literally on the other side; I would have given up the Victory I was waiting for.

Living out the Victory in the BRAVE Life is holding on when all you want to do is let go. When you are at the end of your rope, I encourage you to grab hold tighter and repeat to yourself: *"Change is on the Way because I am refusing to Give Up, I Will Have Victory."*

I want you to understand that victories do not always come in the moments of greatness, the best environments or when we think we will see them. They show up in the trenches, the hard times, when we are in darkness and can't see a glimmer of light. Victory shows up when we are not looking because we are so focused on looking for the big victories that we overlook the smaller ones. There is a reason we must celebrate small victories in life, they are the bricks that build the foundation to housing the larger ones that are to come.

I want to leave you with this:
3 Victory tools to use to celebrate the small Victories in your life even in the midst of challenges:
1.   **Our victories are a part of our healing process.** Believe it or not, when we celebrate victories that are not "big," they allow us to reflect on how far we've come and it shows us our growth. Those parts of us that were broken and hurting, we can see the scab forming, thus showing that the healing process has begun and that we are not where we used to be.

2.   **Small victories always turn into bigger ones when they are acknowledged.** When we take the time to look at the small steps, we realize that inches eventually turn into miles. There is no way to experience the miles without the inches being taken first.

3.   **Our small victories train us to be appreciative of what is to come.** When we take the time to appreciate the small things, we are able to sustain and handle the bigger things that come into our

lives. Every victory doesn't show up the way we expect. Sometimes it will be in the darkness of our lives, and sometimes it will be in the chaos. No matter how they show up or how small, they deserve to be celebrated!

Don't Wait for the Big Victories, You are Already Victorious!

Or as Tye Tribett says,

"Don't wait til the Battle is Over, SHOUT NOW"!!

Victory in the B.R.A.V.E. Life
BRAVE Reflective and Journal Questions to Consider...

1. What small victories have you overlooked in your life lately?

_____
_____
_____
_____
_____
_____

2. With those victories, how have you seen them turn into larger ones?

_____
_____
_____
_____
_____

Your BRAVE Thoughts
Use the following pages to write your thoughts about the chapter and how you are going to live **Victorious** in your Life!

_____
_____
_____
_____
_____
_____
_____
_____
_____
_____
_____
_____
_____
_____
_____

_____
_____
_____
_____
_____
_____
_____
_____
_____
_____
_____
_____
_____
_____

VICTORIOUS Declaration

I am VICTORY,
God has the BEST in store for me!
I am VICTORIOUS
God is Forever Covering Me, Always surrounding me.
I am Everything that God has called me to Be.
I HAVE THE VICTORY,
In Life, In My World, and In My Work!
No matter what is facing Me,

I

Will

Have

Victory!

5

BE Empowered

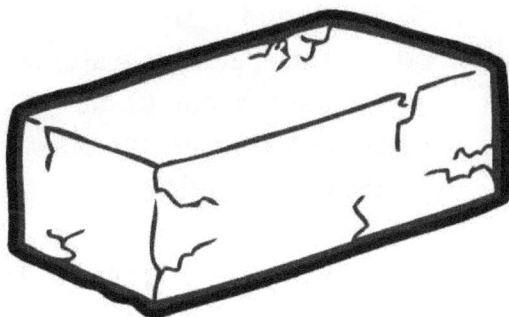

*"Make (someone; **You**) stronger and more confident, especially in controlling their life and claiming their rights. Give (someone; **You**) the Authority or Power to do something "*

Poem
I Got the Power

I didn't see it at the time,
didn't even know I had it
It was clouded by storms, black smoke, and mire

In disguise, it hid itself because I had work to do
I couldn't see it
It came about in the midst of my struggle
It wouldn't have accepted its truth

In the glimmer of light, presented as hope
I started to see
that the power I desperately searched for
was already inside of me
It wasn't until I saw myself
deep in the mirror

I saw the light shine from within and realized all the while

I already
Have
The POWER!

Empowered to Empower

"Let no one despise you for your youth, but set the believers an example in speech, in conduct, in love, in faith, in purity."
1 Timothy 4:12

I never understood why God had chosen me to do what I have been called to do. Honestly, I felt and sometimes still feel inadequate and unqualified for such a task. I mean, let's face it, if you look at my life and look at all the things I have done and the things I struggled with, I would be the least qualified to tell anyone how to live, what to do, and how to do it. Essentially, that is the precise reason I am qualified to do so! I have done it all, made all the mistakes and I can teach and tell you why NOT to make the same choices and if you do, I can tell you how to get out of them. Most often though, as God was shaping me and molding me, I often felt like a hypocrite because I would be telling people to trust God but when I faced a real challenge in life, I would cry out to God and ask Him. "Why me Lord?" I know I am not alone in that.

Many people will not tell you that. They will not be honest with you and tell you how it really is because they were once where you were; scared, afraid, and feeling inadequate. Some people will and those are people who make the biggest impact. Those are the ones who are not afraid to tell the truth at the risk of looking weak and powerless.

Powerlessly Empowered

I remember being a new graduate and I was living with my birth mom. That season of my life was very challenging. I had to live with a woman that I felt I barely knew and I didn't realize I had so much animosity for her. During that time, God used it to show me some things about myself that I did not think I was ready for but it was purposed to prepare me for what I was going to do in the future.

One day, in 2008, I was on the couch laying there, sort of praying but thinking at the same time. The night before I was out with a guy and needless to say, it wasn't a completely holy night. I began to ask God, "Why do I always put myself in these situations? What is wrong with me? I know I am saved but this part of me I cannot shake off." I laid down for a moment and something dropped in my spirit. The word "sexy" came to my mind. Now at first, I thought it was me but then the meaning was different. I wrote down what I heard. "SESI—She Exercises Sexual Integrity." I thought about it and looked at it and thought again.

I sat up and asked God "What is this? What am I supposed to do with this?" He then began to tell me, this was a part of what I was supposed to do and empower others to do the same. I was so excited because I was thinking that this was the way I would stop making these choices myself and at the same time help others that struggled the way I did. What I had not considered was that, just because God gave me something at that time didn't mean it would start right then and there! How many times do we get a great idea or a God-Idea and run with it? Sometimes yes, He will give us something and we are to just go! Other times, it has to grow within us first before we start it, and that was my process.

After God had spoken "SESI" to me, I took it and ran with it. I started gathering women, had my first meeting, and began to plan to have it incorporated into a 501 c3, as I was serious about this. I would have Bible studies, prayer conference calls, I did it all. All the while I still faced my own set of challenges and shortcomings. After a while, it became so frequent that I questioned the very thing God had spoken to me. In all that, my mentor spoke some raw truth to me that I had no choice but to face. It wasn't until I had my daughter that I realized that, God spoke something in me that was to "come to pass" but not for *right now*. I faced the challenging truth of me having to grow into this particular calling, and I was devastated. I felt powerless and defeated, I questioned myself on how I was going to empower anyone when I did not have the power within myself to change for good.

In that moment, God brought me to this scripture,

But the Lord said to Samuel, "Do not consider his appearance or his height, for I have rejected him. The Lord does not look at the things people look at. People look at the outward appearance, but the Lord looks at the heart" (1 Samuel 16:7).

According to study and theologians, David was anointed at the age of 15 years old but he did not reign as king until he was 30 years old. That's FIFTEEN YEARS! Did you read that? FIFTEEN YEARS! I put that in all caps because I want you to understand that just because God called you to it right now doesn't mean you will DO it RIGHT NOW!

David had some growing up to do; he had some character building to grow into before he became the king that God destined him to be. He had to get somethings out of him before God could use him the way he needed to be used.

It's the same with you and me who have been called and chosen. Sometimes, we are anointed but we have to wait to be appointed. Even in that, I want you to understand that just because you are not walking in the manifestation of it, does not mean you are not equipped and you do not have the power inside of you already! It just needs to be developed and that takes time.

Your Empowered Heart

What I love about the scripture regarding David *(and David is one of my favorite people in the Bible and when I get married, and IF I have a son, I want his name to be David. Just FYI to my soon to be husband lol)* is that God prepped Samuel BEFORE going to anoint David. He told him specifically,
"Do not consider his OUTWARD appearance of his HEIGHT *(all physical features).* **For I the Lord do not look at the things people look at. People look at the outward appearance, but the Lord looks at The HEART"** *(God is concerned about what is INSIDE of you that will make the biggest impact)* **- Samuel 16:7**

What is in your heart?

There is Power in your heart, there is a push in your heart, there is Purpose in your heart, and there is Passion in your heart. God is not looking at the fact that you are STILL struggling with sleeping around with men, the fact that you are trying to measure up to others, the fact that you still have unforgiveness against those that hurt you, He is looking at your heart. He is looking at the *you* whom you cannot see yet but He knows it's there. He knows what you have to go through to truly walk in what He already sees in your heart, so it's just a matter of you accepting and trusting what He says about you.

Living BRAVE when Life challenges your Empowerment

There is a reason that empowerment is at the end of living The BRAVE Life. It's the very thing that ties in all that you will have to become in order to live BRAVE to the fullest. It is also the hardest to accept because throughout your life, you may have felt everything but empowered. You may have or may be feeling inadequate, doubtful, fearful, shameful, and just plain powerless. You may even ask yourself, "How can someone LIKE ME be empowered to do anything?" My question to you is, "Who are you not to be?"

Your Feelings are NOT Facts!

One of my sister friends loves to remind me that "feelings are not facts." She tells me this in those times when I am not feeling like who God called me to be. Whenever I "feel" defeated and I make a bad choice, I start to "feel" as though I am not called to reach others because of my mistakes. I "feel" like no one is going to want to listen to me because they will think I am a hypocrite. Whenever I vent and tell her my "feelings," she reminds me that they are NOT facts and she reassures me of what God says about me and the call on my life. So I am going to tell you the same thing. Your "Feelings are NOT Facts." Do not trust how you Feel but trust what You BELIEVE and from WHOM you Believed it!

When life tries to steal the empowerment from you, it will always remind you of your mistakes, what you are not capable of, and the obstacles you are now facing. In those moments, you have to tell yourself and remind yourself of who you are and "whose" you are. You are a child of God and He has called you for such a time as this.

God has given you everything you need to live a holy life, an abundant life, a purpose-filled life and a life that has the ability and capacity to impact and inspire others in a positive way.

Let me leave you with this:
3 Empowerment tools to use to change your perspective when life

challenges your Power within

1.   **Renew your mind and everything negative you have told yourself about yourself.** Yes, you have messed up in life, yes, you struggle at times but you are NOT who you used to be. You have to daily claim the new *you* and constantly give yourself new information. That comes from the word of God and speaking positive things in your life.

(If you are not saved or Christian, I invite you to revisit the BOLD chapter and at the end of the chapter, you can follow the prototype prayer of faith required to accept Jesus Christ as your Lord and Savior and get started with renewing your mind!)

2.   **Start saying positive affirmations in the morning to start your day with reminding yourself of who you are before the world tries to tell you who you are not!** One that you can start saying is, "I am a child of God. He has made me the head and not the tail, I am above and not beneath. He has chosen and called me for greatness and I have been created to inspire those He specifically assigned to me. I am EMPOWERED, ANOINTED and Have been APPOINTED for such a time as This!"

3.   **Live as though you are empowered!** Sometimes, we say things about ourselves but our lives do not add up to it. I challenge you to Live as though you are who God says you are. I challenge you to Live as though you are Empowered to Inspire people. Your life has so much meaning; so much Power and people are waiting for you to show up! Even in your storms, you are being Empowered to Empower.

Empowerment in The B.R.A.V.E. Life
BRAVE Thoughts and Reflective Questions to consider
1. What are you empowered to do?

_____
_____
_____
_____
_____
_____

_____

2. What tries to keep you from living out an empowered BRAVE Life?

_____
_____
_____
_____
_____

Your BRAVE Thoughts

Use the following pages to write your thoughts about the chapter and how you are going to live **Empowered** in your Life!

_____
_____
_____
_____
_____
_____
_____
_____
_____
_____
_____
_____
_____
_____

_____
_____
_____
_____
_____
_____
_____
_____
_____
_____
_____
_____
_____
_____
_____
_____
_____
_____
_____
_____
_____
_____

EMPOWERED Declaration

"I am a child of God. He has made me the head and not the tail, I am above and not beneath. He has chosen and called me for greatness and I have been created to inspire those He specifically assigned to me. I am EMPOWERED, ANOINTED and Have been APPOINTED for such a time as This."

Your
BRAVE Life
Starts
NOW!

❖ **Thank You!**
❖ **The Building Bricks of BRAVE**
❖ **The Building BRAVE Journal**
❖ **About The Author**
❖ **Connect with Takima**

THANK YOU!

Words cannot literally express my sincere thanks and gratitude for you reading my SECOND book! I cannot believe that I wrote another book and that it is in your hands. I can think back to when I was in elementary school. I was in the third grade and I did a writing assignment that led me to the path of writing. Since the third grade, I knew I would be a writer and that became my dream, to be a famous writer. Although I am far from famous, I am connected to those who have been divinely assigned to me, to read my words to be inspired and forever transformed.

Thank you for being inspired by my story and what God has put in me to give to you. I am FOREVER grateful for you! I believe that this book has challenged you, inspired you, and provoked you to live Bold, Resilient, Authentic, Victorious, & Empowered despite what you face in life!

The Building Bricks of B.R.A.V.E

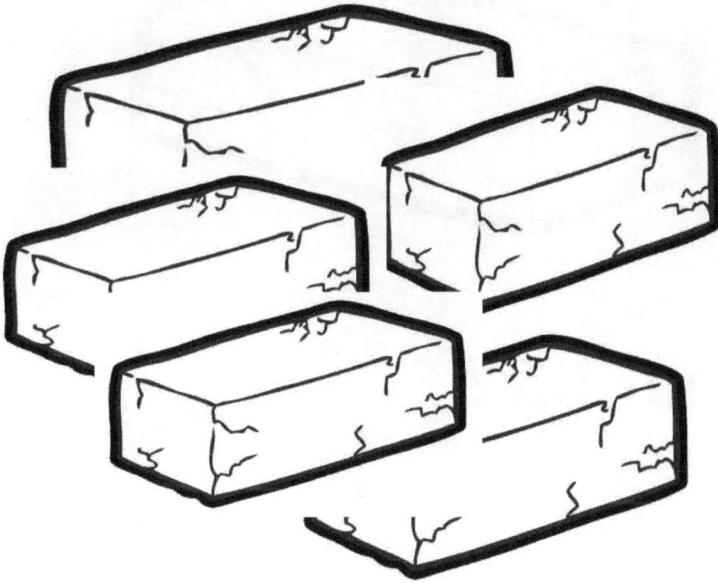

BOLD
RESILIENT
AUTHENTIC
VICTORIOUS
EMPOWERED

How will you lay the Brick of BOLDNESS

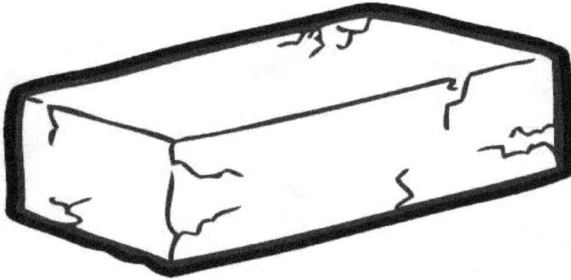

in your life?

I Will...

_____

_____

_____

I Will...

_____

_____

_____

and I Will Always

_____

_____

and Be BOLD and Never Shrink Back!

How will you lay the Brick of RESILIENCE

in your life?

I Will...

_____
_____
_____

I Will...

_____
_____
_____

and I Will Always

_____

and Be RESILIENT and Never GIVE UP!

How will you lay the Brick of AUTHENTCITY

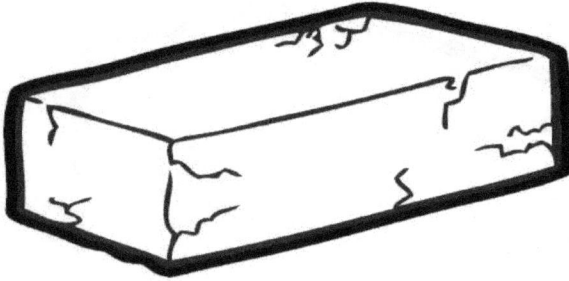

in your life?

I Will...

_____
_____
_____

I Will...

_____
_____
_____

and I Will Always

_____
and Be AUTHENTIC and Always   Be Me!

How will you lay the Brick of VICTORY

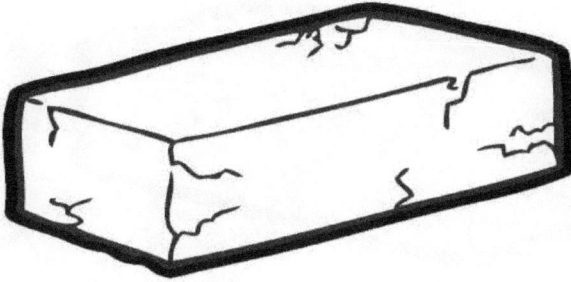

in your life?

I Will...

_____

_____

_____

I Will...

_____

_____

_____

and I Will Always

_____

___

and Be VICTORIOUS and Celebrate EVERY Victory in my Life!

How will you lay the Brick of EMPOWERMENT

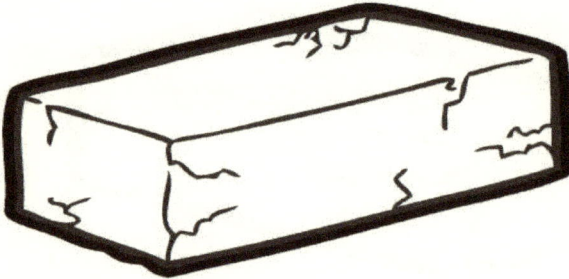

in your life?

I Will...

_____
_____
_____

I Will...

_____
_____
_____

and I Will Always

_____

and Be EMPOWERED!

My BRAVE Life Journal

My name is:

_____

and I am ONE BRAVE

_____
_____ **!**

This is Your BRAVE Life, Journal style!

Journaling is a way to express yourself and release things that you may not be able to express verbally. It is very therapeutic and can be a healing agent in your life. The reason I write and love it so much is that, this is how I started, I journaled. I wrote every time I was upset, I was facing a challenge, I was afraid, I was happy, or I was proud; whatever I was experiencing, I wrote it.

On the following pages, I would like for you to use them to begin to journal. Make use of the bricks of life that were thrown at you to build Your BRAVE Life!

The journal pages will have little prompts to get you started and will end with short BRAVE affirmations.

THE BRAVE LIFE

Lastly, you will have an opportunity to write a letter to yourself. You may be in the middle of a storm right now but I want you to know you will BRAVE THROUGH it!

Your letter will be an encouragement to you and motivation to keep pushing and pulling through. Read it every time you feel like giving up!

Happy Writing, Building and Journaling,
Your BRAVE Life!

My BRAVE Life is BOLD
"Don't be ashamed of the story that will inspire others" - Unknown

Today, I was BOLD when...

_____
_____
_____
_____
_____
_____
_____
_____
_____
_____
_____
_____
_____
_____
_____
_____
_____
_____

THE BRAVE LIFE

My BRAVE Life is BOLD

"Be BRIGHT, Be BRAVE, Be BOLD, Be BEAUTIFUL, Be BRILLIANT" - Karen Kostyla

Today, I was BOLD when...

_____

_____

_____

_____

_____

_____

_____

_____

_____

_____

_____

_____

_____

_____

_____

_____

_____

_____

_____

_____

_____

_____

_____

THE BRAVE LIFE

My BRAVE Life is RESILIENT

"I don't want to be perfect. I only aim to be fearless and RESILIENT and Myself" - Unknown

Today, I was RESILENT when...

_____
_____
_____
_____
_____
_____
_____
_____
_____
_____
_____
_____
_____
_____
_____
_____
_____
_____
_____
_____
_____
_____
_____
_____

My BRAVE Life is RESILIENT

"She stood in the storm, and when the wind did not blow her away, she adjusted her sails" - Elizabeth Edwards

Today, I was RESILENT when...

_____
_____
_____
_____
_____
_____
_____
_____
_____
_____
_____
_____
_____
_____
_____
_____
_____
_____
_____
_____
_____
_____
_____
_____

My BRAVE Life is AUTHENTIC

"By choosing to be our most authentic and loving self, we leave a trail of magic everywhere we go" - Emmanuel

Today, I was AUTHENTIC when...

_____
_____
_____
_____
_____
_____
_____
_____
_____
_____
_____
_____
_____
_____
_____
_____
_____
_____
_____
_____
_____
_____
_____
_____

THE BRAVE LIFE

_____
_____
_____
_____
_____
_____
_____
_____
_____
_____
_____
_____
_____
_____
_____
_____
_____
_____
_____
_____
_____
_____
_____
_____

My BRAVE Life is AUTHENTIC

"If you're your AUTHENTIC self, you will have no competition" - Unknown

Today, I was AUTHENTIC when...

_____
_____
_____
_____
_____
_____
_____
_____
_____
_____
_____
_____
_____
_____
_____
_____
_____
_____
_____
_____
_____
_____
_____

My BRAVE Life is VICTORIOUS

"You were never created to live depressed, defeated, guilty, condemned, ashamed, or unworthy. You were created to be VICTORIOUS" - Unknown

Today, I was VICTORIOUS when...

_____

_____

_____

_____

_____

_____

_____

_____

_____

_____

_____

_____

_____

_____

_____

_____

_____

_____

_____

_____

_____

_____

My BRAVE Life is VICTORIOUS

"Be Strong when you are weak, Brave when you are scared and Humble when you are VICTORIOUS" - Unknown

Today, I was VICTORIOUS when...

_____

_____

_____

_____

_____

_____

_____

_____

_____

_____

_____

_____

_____

_____

_____

_____

_____

_____

_____

_____

_____

_____

_____

_____
_____
_____
_____
_____
_____
_____
_____
_____
_____
_____
_____
_____
_____
_____
_____
_____
_____
_____
_____
_____
_____
_____
_____
_____

My BRAVE Life is EMPOWERED

"The most liberating and EMPOWERING day of my life was the day I freed myself from my own self-destructive nonsense"
- Steve Maraboli

Today, I was EMPOWERED when...

_____
_____
_____
_____
_____
_____
_____
_____
_____
_____
_____
_____
_____
_____
_____
_____
_____
_____
_____
_____
_____
_____
_____

THE BRAVE LIFE

_____
_____
_____
_____
_____
_____
_____
_____
_____
_____
_____
_____
_____
_____
_____
_____
_____
_____
_____
_____
_____
_____

My BRAVE Letter

Below, I want you to write a letter to yourself that speaks to how BRAVE you are, because YOU ARE! Even if you do not "feel" BRAVE right now, speak to how you WANT to be BRAVE.

Dear _____,
* Put your name on the line *

You have been through some real _____ in your life, but you _____
_____
_____
_____.

You are Bold because
_____
_____
_____

You are Resilient because
_____
_____
_____

You are Authentic because

_____
_____
_____

You are Victorious because

_____
_____
_____

You are Empowered because
_____
_____
_____

You are BRAVE! I am SO

_____

THE BRAVE LIFE

I Love You!

Love, _____

ABOUT TAKIMA

Takima Howze is a writer, inspirational speaker and the founder/creator of The BRAVE Life™. Takima is passionate about transforming people's lives through her words and stories of triumph through trials.

Takima is a Master Workshop Facilitator who teaches her participants how to look into the mirrors of self and push past the Fear, Struggle and Frustration to become Bold, Resilient, Authentic, Victorious, & Empowered in their Lives!

Takima is also a blogger and independent author who desires to write books and blogs that inspire people to Live BRAVE to change their world. Takima has but one motto and that has become her Signature life message,

"Be You, Stay True and Live B.R.A.V.E!"
Be BRAVE ALWAYS

Love,
Takima Howze!

Connect with me on Social Media:
Facebook:
@TakimaHowze
www.facebook.com/takima.howze

Instagram:
@Takimahwrites

Periscope:
@Takimahwrites

Email Me ANYTIME:
takima@takimahwrites.com